STAR WARS™
WHERE'S THE WOOKIEE?

EGMONT

We bring stories to life

First published in Great Britain 2016 by Egmont UK Limited
The Yellow Building, 1 Nicholas Road, London W11 4AN

Illustrations by Ulises Farinas
Colour by Ryan Hill
Written by Katrina Pallant
Designed by Richie Hull

© & ™ 2016 Lucasfilm Ltd.
ISBN 978 1 4052 8419 6
64142/1
Printed in Italy

To find more great *Star Wars* books, visit www.egmont.co.uk/starwars

Stay safe online. Any website addresses listed in this book are correct at the time of going to print. However, Egmont is not responsible for content hosted by third parties. Please be aware that online content can be subject to change and websites can contain content that is unsuitable for children. We advise that all children are supervised when using the internet.

WANTED

FOR CRIMES AGAINST THE EMPIRE

DEAD
OR ALIVE

REWARD
725,000

CHEWBACCA

This rebel is the number one prize. Despite his towering height and distinctive smell, he is an expert at evading capture.

HAN SOLO

Not to be overshadowed by his mammoth co-pilot, this charming smuggler is well-known for his criminal activity. Where there's a Chewie, Han won't be far away.

MILLENNIUM FALCON

Home to Han and Chewie, this famous freighter is lightning-fast and rarely at port. If it's not in hyperspace, you might be able to spot it.

GREEDO

Short-tempered and overconfident, this unlucky Rodian was never the most skilled bounty hunter. Chewie shouldn't have too much trouble avoiding this guy.

BOBA FETT

The most notorious bounty hunter in the universe is on Chewie's trail. Beating him to the bounty will not be easy.

THE HUNT IS ON!

Find these characters in every location

DENGAR

This Corellian is held in high regard for his excellent track record of hunting down his mark. Look out for his turban and plated armour.

BOSSK

A fierce warrior and hunter, Bossk is renowned and feared for his success in the Clone Wars. He carries a large mortar gun that fires high impact bolts.

ZUCKUSS

This insectoid is from the planet Gand. You wouldn't want to come face-to-face with this skilled bounty hunter.

4-LOM

Often employed by the Galactic Empire, this former protocol droid is an expert in hunting down rebel activity.

IG-88

This bounty hunter was once an IG-series assassin droid. Watch out for those sensors, because this droid is fierce competition.

LOCATIONS

✛ Hunt Chewie throughout the galaxy!

Chewie has a sizeable bounty on his head. Rarely seen without his partner-in-crime, Han Solo, this Wookiee has evaded capture on multiple occasions. They make their escape on the fastest freighter in the galaxy, the *Millennium Falcon*.

Can you find this furry criminal before other accomplished bounty hunters beat you to it? These are the locations that Chewie has been known to hide.

JAWA MARKET

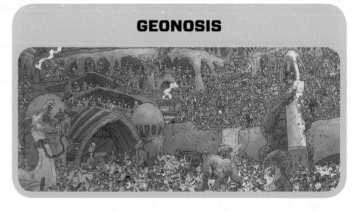

HOTH

GEONOSIS

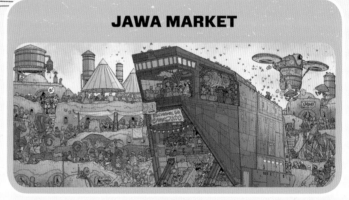

CORUSCANT

MOS EISLEY

STAR DESTROYER

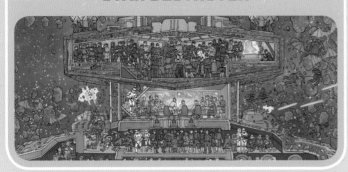

CLOUD CITY

ECHO BASE

THE CANTINA

EWOK VILLAGE

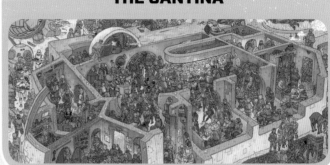

JEDI TEMPLE

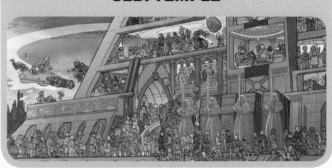

THE DEATH STAR

JABBA'S PALACE

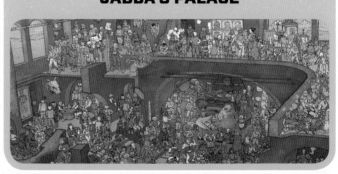

IMPERIAL HANGAR

KASHYYYK

JAWA MARKET

The Jawas are in town with some droids to sell. Residents of Tatooine and beyond gather to grab themselves a bargain from these scavengers. Rebels know this is the place to find parts to repair their mechanical companions.

HOTH

Many a battle has been fought between the rebels and Imperials in this dramatic snowscape. The two sides bring their greatest firepower and soldiers to defend their cause, but they have to watch out for Hoth's local predators!

GEONOSIS

In the Outer Rim, on the desert planet of Geonosis, there lives a winged, insectoid species. Geonosians enjoy gladiatorial-style entertainment, with great beasts fighting it out in the famous arena.

CORUSCANT

This bustling Imperial city is seen as the centre of Galactic culture. As the home of the Imperial government and the Emperor himself, it's the last place you'd expect to find enemies of the Empire ...

MOS EISLEY

A busy day in the marketplace draws visitors from all over the universe. Described once as a "hive of scum and villainy", Mos Eisley plays host to smugglers, black-market traders and all-round criminal activity – the perfect hiding place for rebels.

STAR DESTROYER

This heavily-armed warship sails through the stars pursuing the rebels. Aboard are the most terrifying commanders in the Imperial fleet, plus a few unlikely visitors.

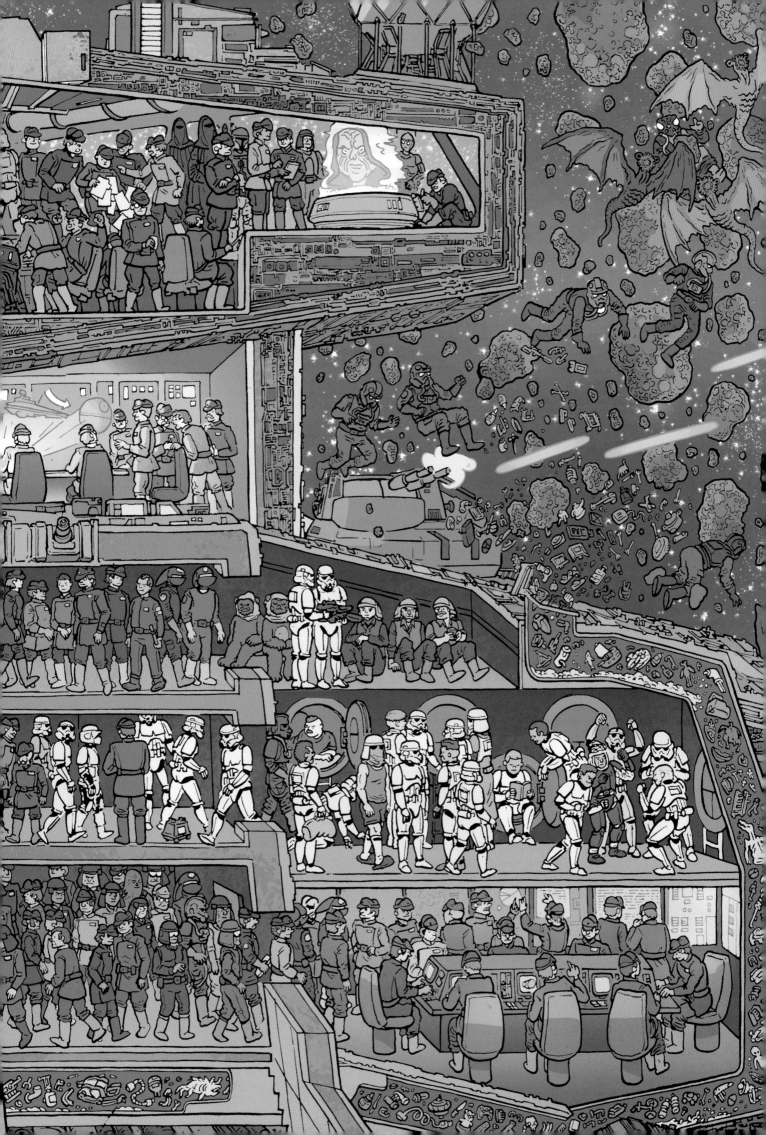

CLOUD CITY

In the sky above the planet Bespin there is a mining colony surrounded by clouds. Relatively unimportant to the Empire's plans, the city allows rebels to blend in and stay hidden. Or so the rebels think.

ECHO BASE

On the unforgiving plains of Hoth the rebels have found a refuge from the Empire. The base is protected by a deflector shield, and an ion cannon deters any unwanted visitors.

THE CANTINA

This fine establishment is a great place for spacers to enjoy a beverage, listen to music and engage in a fist-fight. It is an ideal spot for outlaws to pick up work, but it can also attract the attention of master bounty hunters.

EWOK VILLAGE

Up in the trees of Endor there lives a tribe of the most curious, furry creatures in the galaxy. Bright Tree Village is home to some brave Ewoks who, whilst appearing cute and small, are fierce when defending their kingdom.

JEDI TEMPLE

Home to the Jedi Order, Younglings are trained here in the ways of the Force. A spot of lightsaber training, a chat with the Jedi Council or a browse through the Jedi Archives are popular pastimes. Friends are welcome, unless you're a Sith.

THE DEATH STAR

Aboard the most powerful weapon in the universe, droids are hard at work, stormtroopers are preparing for battle, and operations to attack a rebel base are in full swing. Little do the Imperial forces know that the most notorious rebels are already in their midst.

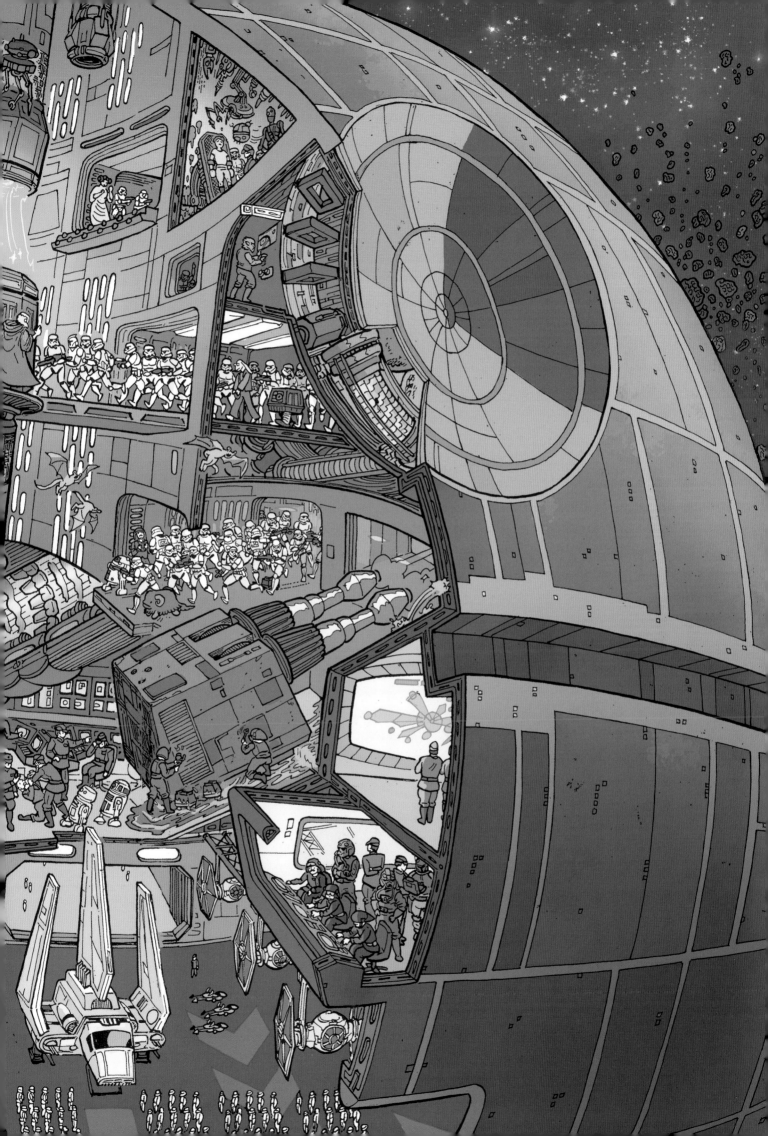

JABBA'S PALACE

In the Dune Sea on Tatooine there lives a notorious crime lord named Jabba the Hutt. Jabba controls most of Tatooine's illegal operations, and his palace is often occupied by underworld characters. Bounty hunters find fortune here collecting debts for Jabba.

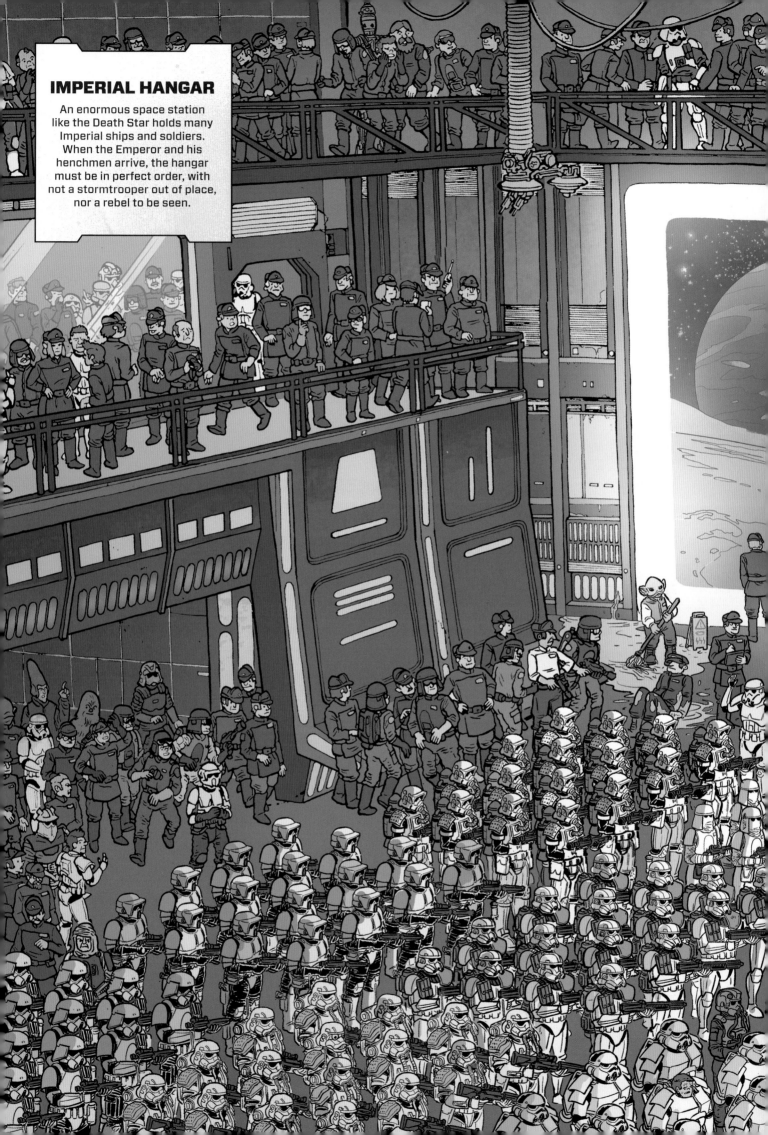

IMPERIAL HANGAR

An enormous space station like the Death Star holds many Imperial ships and soldiers. When the Emperor and his henchmen arrive, the hangar must be in perfect order, with not a stormtrooper out of place, nor a rebel to be seen.

KASHYYYK

Homeworld to the mighty Wookiee race, Kashyyyk is a dangerous place for enemies. These powerful, loyal and hairy creatures are ready for a fight, especially in protecting one of their own.

GALACTIC CHECKLIST

These might be a bit harder to find ...

JAWA MARKET

- [ ] A Jawa feeding the birds
- [ ] Stormtrooper looking for R2-D2
- [ ] Falling Jawa
- [ ] Helmet shopper
- [ ] R5-D4
- [ ] A PIT droid
- [ ] Herd of nuna "swamp turkeys"
- [ ] An astromech strapped to a bantha
- [ ] A droid with a pincer hand
- [ ] One-eyed Jawa
- [ ] An acklay

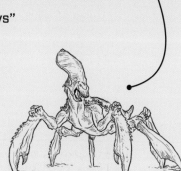

HOTH

- [ ] A fearless Jedi
- [ ] A rebel on an Imperial speeder bike
- [ ] A rebel headfirst in the snow
- [ ] A snowball fight
- [ ] A wampa
- [ ] Rebel on a tauntaun
- [ ] 3 bungee-jumping Imperials
- [ ] Three X-wing pilots
- [ ] Rebel and snowtrooper in hand-to-hand combat
- [ ] Rebel wielding two blaster pistols
- [ ] Blue Mon Calamari

GEONOSIS

- [ ] Fighting Huttlet
- [ ] Wampa
- [ ] Droid with a warhammer
- [ ] Weapons bin
- [ ] Gungan warrior posse
- [ ] A guarlara (Naboo horse)
- [ ] Viking astromech
- [ ] One-eyed Wookiee
- [ ] Two wrestlers
- [ ] Two tough Jawas
- [ ] Two baby Geonosians
- [ ] An Ewok spectator
- [ ] An Amani archer
- [ ] 2 nexu
- [ ] 2 anoobas

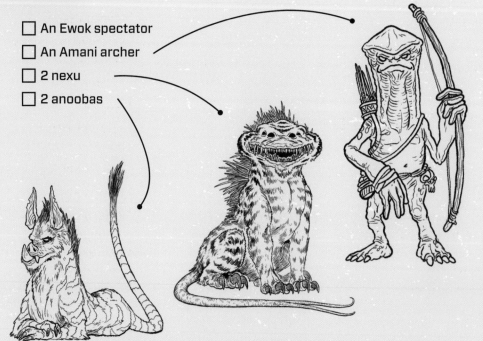

CORUSCANT

- [ ] Someone enjoying the scene through viewpoint binoculars
- [ ] A Star Destroyer
- [ ] Newspaper boy
- [ ] Tourist with a dog
- [ ] A Jedi falling
- [ ] A Jawa
- [ ] The Death Star
- [ ] A Gran

MOS EISLEY

- [ ] A graffiti artist
- [ ] Baby dianoga
- [ ] Luke's landspeeder
- [ ] Garindan the Imperial spy
- [ ] Watto
- [ ] Clumsy Ortolan knocking a woman off the balcony
- [ ] Jawa pickpocketing
- [ ] Jawas stealing cable
- [ ] Jabba the Hutt receiving a new pet rancor
- [ ] Dug nomad trader

STAR DESTROYER

- [ ] An unwanted games console controller
- [ ] A discarded chicken
- [ ] Two Ewoks
- [ ] Troopers in a fist fight
- [ ] AT-ST hologram
- [ ] 1 scout trooper
- [ ] The Emperor
- [ ] Mynocks
- [ ] A mouse droid
- [ ] A black astromech
- [ ] Imperial officer dropping a folder of important papers
- [ ] Imperial officer fixing a holo-projector
- [ ] A Bothan officer
- [ ] Darth Vader's helmet
- [ ] 2 Ugnaughts

CLOUD CITY

- [ ] Man who dropped his briefcaase
- [ ] Air traffic controller
- [ ] 3 yellow birds
- [ ] Mechanic who has dropped his tools
- [ ] A happy dog
- [ ] A Jawa
- [ ] An alien with a bunch of flowers
- [ ] Lando Calrissian
- [ ] Darth Vader
- [ ] Wookiee in sunglasses
- [ ] Garindan the Imperial spy

ECHO BASE

- [ ] Yoda wearing a woolly coat
- [ ] Hot drinks cart
- [ ] Doughnuts
- [ ] Foam peanuts
- [ ] A speeder being polished
- [ ] Unhappy Ewoks
- [ ] A Mon Calamari
- [ ] Shield Generator
- [ ] Rebel with a fire extinguisher
- [ ] R2-D2
- [ ] Two Gonk droids
- [ ] R5 unit

THE CANTINA

- [ ] Baby Hutt
- [ ] Man trapped by sarlacc
- [ ] Clumsy speederbike rider
- [ ] Graffiti artist
- [ ] Gungan dancer
- [ ] Figrin D'an playing a merry tune
- [ ] A clock
- [ ] A dartboard
- [ ] A stormtrooper helmet
- [ ] Super battle droid
- [ ] A dice game
- [ ] A card game
- [ ] An angry chess player
- [ ] A Bith who has lost his glasses

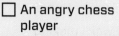

EWOK VILLAGE

- [ ] Ewok on a swing
- [ ] Ewok couple enjoying the fire
- [ ] A person drying off after an unwanted dip
- [ ] Ewok family sunbathing
- [ ] Ewok king
- [ ] Ewok carrying a pot on its head
- [ ] A sleepy lizard
- [ ] A photo opportunity
- [ ] Ewok with a winged headband
- [ ] Ewok in a bowler hat
- [ ] A leaping fish
- [ ] Ewok wearing a straw hat
- [ ] A geejaw bird resting on a stump

JEDI TEMPLE

- [ ] Younglings learning the Force
- [ ] Yoda
- [ ] A Padawan assembling her lightsaber
- [ ] A two-headed Jedi
- [ ] A statue with a moustache
- [ ] A bandage-wrapped alien
- [ ] A Jawa
- [ ] Sith Lord battling a Jedi
- [ ] Three Jedi Ewoks
- [ ] Boushh the bounty hunter

THE DEATH STAR

- [ ] 3 Royal Guards
- [ ] Ewoks making their escape
- [ ] A Gungan under arrest
- [ ] Imperials enjoying a movie
- [ ] A frustrated thirsty TIE fighter pilot
- [ ] Two soggy mouse droids
- [ ] A cat poster
- [ ] A snoozing stormtrooper
- [ ] Obi-Wan Kenobi
- [ ] Princess Leia
- [ ] C-3PO
- [ ] R2-D2
- [ ] Mother and child space slugs

JABBA'S PALACE

- [ ] Hidden treasure stash
- [ ] Dianoga in a toilet
- [ ] Baby opee-sea killer (fishcrab from Naboo)
- [ ] Jawa with a pet scurrier
- [ ] Young Anakin Skywalker ready for a podrace
- [ ] Monk of the B'omarr Order

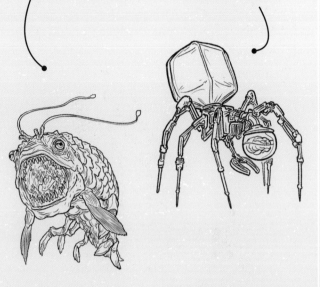

IMPERIAL HANGAR

- [ ] An important visitor
- [ ] Droid mechanic
- [ ] A janitor
- [ ] An Imperial taking a photo
- [ ] Mouse droid
- [ ] A Mon Calamari officer
- [ ] Snowtrooper being inspected
- [ ] A duck-headed trooper
- [ ] Stormtrooper being inspected
- [ ] Power droid

KASHYYYK

- [ ] Yoda in a fight
- [ ] Jedi Wookiee
- [ ] General Grievous
- [ ] Wookiee wearing a Fedora
- [ ] Geonosian
- [ ] Wookiee wearing a hooded cloak
- [ ] An Ewok
- [ ] Wookiee with Leia's hairstyle
- [ ] Squad of Trandoshans

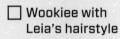

THE HUNT CONTINUES ...